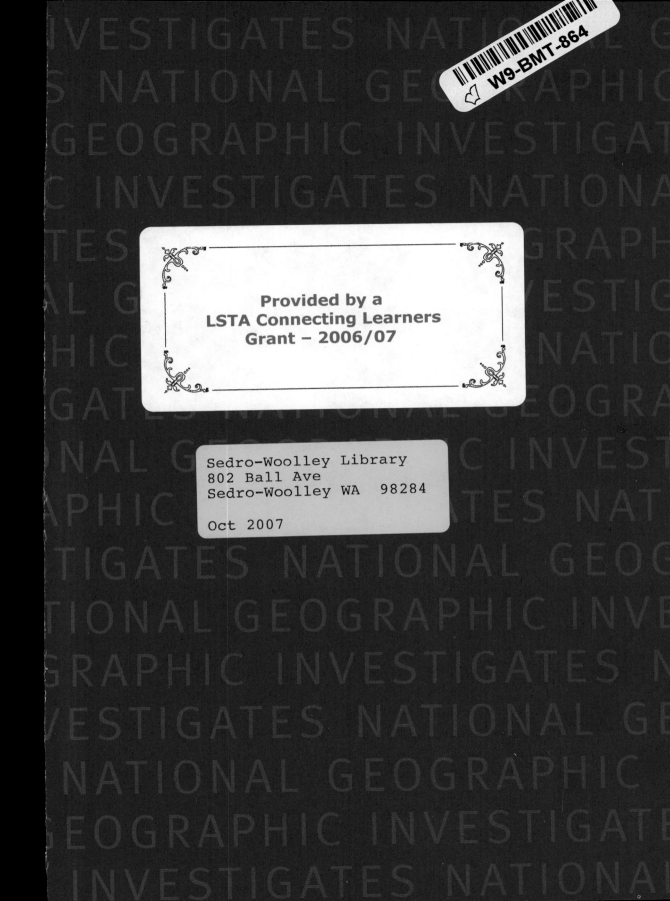

Ancient Iraq

Archaeology Unlocks the Secrets of Iraq's Past

By Beth Gruber

Tony Wilkinson, Consultant

NATIONAL GEOGRAPHIC

Washington, DC

Contents

< This bas-relief shows the Assyrian king Ashurnasirpal II, who ruled in the ninth century B.C. It decorated his palace in the city of Nimrud.

< Many of Iraq's great monuments date to the early Islamic era. This minaret is found at Samarra and was built in the ninth century A.D.

Ancient Mesopotamia: the first cities, the first writing, perhaps the earliest civilization. This book shows just why ancient Iraq is important, not only for the people of Iraq, but also for the entire world.

What excites me about Mesopotamian archaeology is the sense of discovery that is always present. In the deserts between the Tigris and Euphrates rivers are the remains of thousands of villages, towns, and cities. It is the job of the archaeologist to protect and record these sites and the landscape in which they stand. Not only do they reveal the history of the earliest civilizations, they also help us to understand how our own societies came about.

The fascinating story told in this book is just the tip of the iceberg. Much more remains—not just in the ground but also in the records of nearly 200 years of research. Archaeological surveys, the analysis of texts and satellite images, and traditional excavation have all contributed to the process of discovery, but this unique record will not remain for long unless it is protected. Iraqi archaeologists and their colleagues from the international community have the difficult task of trying to preserve it amid the present-day turmoil. This book will enable you to appreciate this dramatic and evolving story.

T. J. Wilkinson

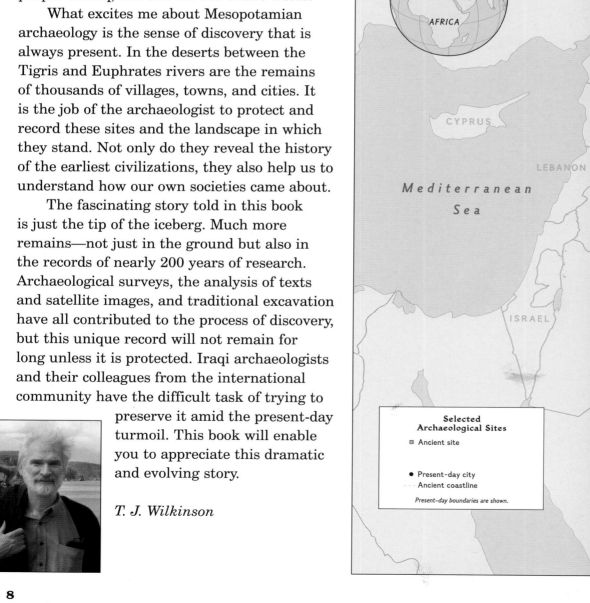

Ancient Iraq

EUROPE   ASIA

AFRICA

CYPRUS

LEBANON

Mediterranean Sea

ISRAEL

Selected Archaeological Sites

▪ Ancient site

● Present-day city
--- Ancient coastline

Present-day boundaries are shown.

8

Map of Important Iraqi Archaeological Sites

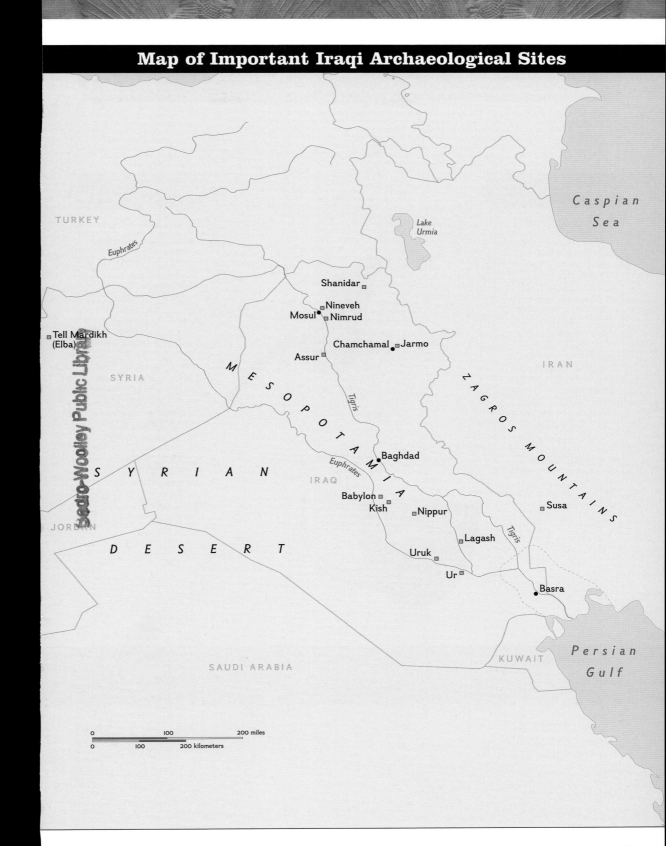

TURKEY

Euphrates

Caspian Sea

Lake Urmia

Shanidar

Nineveh

Mosul • Nimrud

Tell Mardikh (Elba)

Chamchamal • Jarmo

Assur

Tigris

SYRIA

IRAN

M E S O P O T A M I A

Z A G R O S   M O U N T A I N S

S Y R I A N

Euphrates

Baghdad

IRAQ

JORDAN

Babylon

Kish

Nippur

Susa

D E S E R T

Lagash

Tigris

Uruk

Ur

Basra

SAUDI ARABIA

KUWAIT

Persian Gulf

0   100   200 miles

0   100   200 kilometers

THREE MAJOR PERIODS OF
Iraqi History

Sumer

ca 2112–2004 B.C.

Sumer is the name that historians give to the southernmost part of Mesopotamia. From about 3500 B.C. onward it was home to a number of city states, including Ur, Uruk, Lagash, and Nippur. These states were often at war with one another and from time to time one would dominate the others. The map on the right shows the area ruled by Ur at the time of the city's Third Dynasty (ca 2112–2004 B.C.). It was during this period that work began on the famous ziggurat of Ur, one of ancient Mesopotamia's most famous monuments. The dynasty came to an end when Ur fell to the Elamites.

Babylon

ca 1792–1750 B.C.

Babylon was a relatively unimportant city until about 1900 B.C., when it became the center of a small kingdom. In the following years the rulers of Babylon conquered the surrounding city states to create an empire. The map on the right shows the Babylonian empire at the time of Hammurabi, who ruled between about 1792 and 1750 B.C. The influence of Babylon lessened over the following centuries. Another great period of Babylonian power began in the late seventh century B.C. During the reign of Nebuchadnezzar II (ca 605–561 B.C.) the city became famous for its magnificent palaces.

< **This golden goblet was found at Ur in the grave of a queen.**

Timeline of Iraqi History

3500 B.C.

ca 3500 First city states develop in Mesopotamia

Prehistory
ca 60,000 B.C. Neanderthal man known as "Shandy" buried at Shanidar Cave
ca 9000 B.C. Hunter-gatherers first begin to farm
ca 7000 B.C. Settlement founded at Jarmo

3000

ca 3200 Writing develops

2500

ca 2500 Queen Puabi buried at Ur

ca 2334 Sargon of Akkad comes to power; he conquers much of Mesopotamia to create the Akkadian empire

ca 2150 End of Akkadian dynasty

2000

ca 1900 Horse-drawn chariots first used in war

ca 2100 Work begins on the ziggurat at Ur

Assyria

ca 858–824 B.C.

Assyria was a kingdom in northern Mesopotamia that was originally based around the city of Assur. The greatest period in Assyrian history began in the late ninth century B.C. Under warlike kings such as Ashurnasirpal II (ca 883–859 B.C.) and Shalmaneser III (ca 858–824 B.C.) the Assyrians carved out a huge empire. The empire during Shalmaneser's reign is shown on the right. If states that paid tribute were to be included, it would stretch even farther, from the Persian Gulf to the Mediterranean Sea.

> **This ceramic mask, found in an ancient Assyrian city, dates to about 1300 B.C.**

1500

ca 1790 Hammurabi becomes king of Babylon

ca 883 Ashurnasirpal II begins reign; he expands the Assyrian empire and moves its capital to Nimrud

1000

ca 612 Assyrian city of Nineveh falls to Medes and Babylonians

ca 605 Nebuchadnezzar II becomes king of Babylon; his reign marks high point of Babylonian culture

500

ca 539 Babylon falls to Persians

0

Modern Era
1921 Modern state of Iraq established
1932 Iraq becomes independent from Great Britain
1979 Saddam Hussein comes to power
2003 U.S. intervention ends Hussein's reign
2006 Hussein dies by hanging after his trial in an Iraqi court

Yesterday Comes Alive

CHAPTER 1

How do we learn what we know about the past?

What did you do this morning? Take a ride to school by bus? Maybe you read a magazine on the way. Or perhaps you were too busy worrying about the math quiz that was waiting for you when you got there. Whatever you were doing, you probably checked your watch at some time, just to see if you were late.

The wheel. Writing. Mathematics. Even the way that we divide hours into 60 minutes and minutes into 60 seconds. Many of the things that we take for granted today were invented by the people who lived in a region of ancient Iraq. Historians call this

< The ziggurat of Ur stands in the deserts of Iraq. Ziggurats were step-sided pyramids used as temples. This ziggurat was originally built to honor the moon god Nanna in the late 22nd and early 21st centuries B.C.

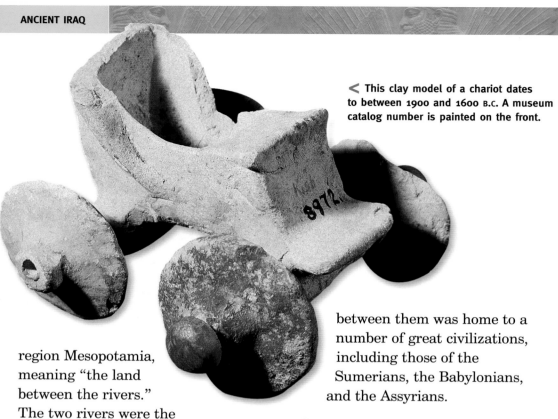

< This clay model of a chariot dates to between 1900 and 1600 B.C. A museum catalog number is painted on the front.

region Mesopotamia, meaning "the land between the rivers." The two rivers were the Tigris and the Euphrates, and from about 3500 B.C. onward, the area between them was home to a number of great civilizations, including those of the Sumerians, the Babylonians, and the Assyrians.

Cities of mud

If you were to look at the landscape of ancient Mesopotamia today, you would see few monuments to rival the pyramids of Egypt, the Parthenon and

V Ferryboats line up on the Tigris River. In ancient times many great cities were built on its banks, including Nineveh and Assur.

< Most buildings in ancient Mesopotamia were made of mud bricks such as these.

V This helmet is made from gold and silver. It was found at Ur in the tomb of King Meskalumdug.

Acropolis of Greece, or Rome's great Colosseum. One reason so little of ancient Iraq remains standing today is that many of its oldest towns were built of mud. Without stone, ancient Iraqis built their homes and temples from piled-up mud or from lumps of clay that they pressed together like bricks. Roofs were made of earth spread over reed mats and tree trunks—wood was in too short supply to make entire houses out of it. Floors were also built of earth, sometimes covered with a soft, white mineral called gypsum. Gypsum was used as a kind of plaster in ancient times.

So how do we know what we know about ancient Iraq and the great civilizations that survived and thrived there for more than 3,000 years?

Telling tales

In the deserts of southern Iraq, huge earth mounds called "tells" contain evidence formed over thousands of years. This evidence comes from the remains of ancient civilizations that have occupied the same location over different periods of time.

During the last century and a half, archaeologists, travelers, and others have dug into these tells and found objects that have given us fascinating glimpses of life in ancient Iraq. Sometimes on purpose, at other times by chance, they have discovered clay tablets covered with mysterious writing. They have also found cylinder seals covered with curious symbols. Thousands of years ago these seals were rolled in wet clay to create the ancient Mesopotamian equivalent of a

Write like a Babylonian

Are you curious about what your initials might have looked like in the cuneiform script used by the ancient Mesopotamians? Thanks to modern technology, it's now easy to find out. First, go to your home computer or a computer at your school, school library media center, or local library. Log on to the Internet and go to http://www.upennmuseum.com/cuneiform.cgi. All you have to do is type in your full name. Then type in your initials, and click "inscribe." The computers at the University of Pennsylvania Museum of Archaeology and Anthropology do the rest! Your monogram will flash on the screen in seconds.

> **This clay tablet is inscribed with cuneiform script. It was found at the ancient city of Lagash.**

V **This cylinder seal would have been rolled in clay to produce the "signature" on the right.**

signature. Archaeologists have also discovered painted murals and even the remains of vast cities, temples, and palaces.

But with thousands of tells scattered from Basra in southern Iraq to Mosul in the north, how does an archaeologist know where to dig? One way to determine what might be in a tell is to carry out a sounding. Some soundings are performed by digging trenches into the surface of the mound at various angles. As the trenches grow deeper, the objects that are found are collected for dating purposes. Sketches, maps, and

photographs are made to show precisely where the objects were found.

Soundings can also be performed by cutting long trenches from the side of a mound to its center, almost like you would cut into a cake. Just like a cake, the sides of the slice have layers. Each one contains evidence from a different period in the site's history, with the most recent objects at the top and the oldest at the bottom.

Tablets that talk

Of all the objects found in Iraq's tells, the ones that have provided us with the most information about ancient Mesopotamia are the countless clay tablets that have been discovered with cuneiform writing on them. Cuneiform was the type of script that the Mesopotamians used. Cuneiform tablets were originally invented for record keeping. The first examples just contained lists of the number of sheep or cattle someone owned. However, the tablets were eventually used to write down laws, historical accounts, stories, scientific texts, and more. Together with inscriptions stamped on bricks used to build temples and palaces, they provide a written record of ancient Iraqi history. Thanks to these records, historians have been able to give us amazing insight into what life was like then.

In the following chapters we will investigate some of the incredible civilizations that have existed in Mesopotamia. We start in chapter 2 by

The world's oldest neighborhood?

Many of Iraq's great ancient cities now consist of little more than ruins in the desert. The days when people carried out their work, shopped, and went to school there are long gone. However, one neighborhood is still home to people today, thousands of years after it was first inhabited. It is the Citadel. Now part of the city of Arbil (also known as Erbil), it is found in the northern Kurdish part of Iraq.

Surrounded by stone walls, the Citadel has been a living neighborhood for at least 7,000 years—and possibly even longer than that. Archaeologists believe that there may have been a settlement of early farmers near the site in about 9000 B.C. In the centuries that followed, the Citadel was home to Sumerians, Akkadians, Assyrians, Persians, and Greeks. Today's residents are sitting on top of thousands of years of archaeological evidence. Will it ever be excavated? No one can say for sure!

looking at some truly ancient history— prehistoric graves that date back as far as 100,000 years. In the following chapter we tell the story of the Sumerians, the inhabitants of a number of powerful city states that thrived from 3500 B.C. onward. Chapters 4 and 5 examine two more great civilizations: Babylon and Assyria. And finally, in chapter 6, we look at some of the huge challenges facing archaeologists in the early 21st century, in the unpredictable and violent times following the downfall of Saddam Hussein's government.

Back to the Stone Age

CHAPTER 2

When did human beings first begin to farm?

It certainly would make an archaeologist's job easier if every artifact he or she found was inscribed with a date. But that is not usually the case. Long before the Sumerians wrote on tablets, in a time before recorded history, Iraq was home to prehistoric humans.

Some of the prehistoric sites in Iraq date back more than 100,000 years. One of the oldest is found at Barda-Balka, located between the modern-day Iraqi cities of Sulaimaniyeh and Kirkuk. In 1949 human remains were discovered there by Dr. Naji al Asil, former director general of the Iraqi

< The Zagros Mountains, which separate Iraq from Iran, are home to several important prehistoric sites.

How old is it?

One of the first things that archaeologists want to know when they find an object is how old it is. Often there are no inscriptions to give them a helping hand. But modern archaeologists have a range of dating techniques available to them.

In the late 19th and early 20th centuries, when many of the most important Mesopotamian discoveries were made, archaeologists used contextual dating techniques. By noting which layer of a site an object came from, they could tell its rough date because it would be older than objects in the layer above and newer than those in the layer below.

In the 1940s the U.S. chemist Willard Libby helped develop a new way of dating objects. He discovered that as time passes, the carbon-14 in certain natural materials such as bone and cloth fibers decays at a rate that can be carefully measured. By noting this rate of decay, archaeologists are able to date an object more accurately.

Other forms of dating include potassium-argon dating, which is used to date very old pieces of rock, and dendrochronology, which involves counting tree rings.

< A sample is taken from a human bone so that it can be dated.

Department of Antiquities. They are believed to be among the oldest human remains in the world. It is estimated that they are 120,000 years old.

In the 1950s, an excavation led by American Dr. Robert J. Braidwood turned up stone tools from the same site. He estimated that they were more than 100,000 years old. When Braidwood loaned the tools to a blood analyst many years later, the scientist discovered that some of the tools were spotted with traces of human blood from the same time period. Was the blood astonishing evidence of a prehistoric murder? Was it proof of human sacrifice? Or did the toolmaker or person using the tool simply cut himself or herself on its sharp edge? We may never know.

Early cavemen

One of the most famous prehistoric archaeological sites in Iraq is Shanidar Cave, which is located in the northernmost tip of the country. Work was first carried out there in 1951 by the U.S. archaeologist Dr. Ralph Solecki. Solecki made his first major discovery two years later—the skeleton of a Neanderthal infant, buried for more than 60,000 years. A second skeleton was unearthed in 1957. This man was initially known as Shanidar 1, but when they were talking among themselves, Solecki and his team referred to him as Nandy—and the name stuck!

When Dr. Solecki and his fellow archaeologists examined the skeleton, they noted its dislocated jaw and badly twisted spine. Further study revealed that Nandy was probably about 40 years old when he died, badly crippled, and at least partially blind. He was missing a portion of his right arm, and his leg was broken. Nandy received most of his injuries before his death, leading Solecki to conclude that he was cared for by the rest of the community in his old age. Many experts were surprised that early humans would show such concern for each other.

Another skeleton found at Shanidar, known as Shanidar 4, offered other hints at life 60,000 years ago. Around the remains of the body were pollen grains from over 20 different types of wildflowers. Because the concentration of pollen was far greater near the body than in other parts of the site, the archaeologists concluded that the flowers were put there as part of a ritual burial. One thing that was especially interesting was the fact that most of the flowers were ones that have traditionally been used for medicinal purposes. So, could Shanidar 4 have been some

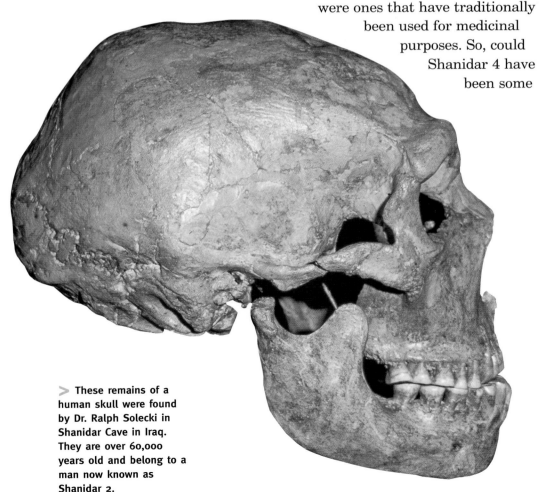

> These remains of a human skull were found by Dr. Ralph Solecki in Shanidar Cave in Iraq. They are over 60,000 years old and belong to a man now known as Shanidar 2.

21

⋀ **Emmer wheat was one of the first crops to be grown by humans. It is shown here both with and without its husk.**

early kind of shaman or medicine man? It certainly is possible. However, since the body was discovered, some experts have suggested that there may be a slightly less interesting explanation. There were a number of animal holes near the graves, and the concentration of pollen could have been the result of rodents storing food.

In 1960 Solecki and his team made another monumental discovery—a 12,000-year-old Neolithic cemetery containing 35 bodies in 26 burial sites. Each site contained what appeared to be funeral gifts for the dead to use in the afterlife. Strings of beads were found inside infant graves, while those for adults contained practical goods such as hunting tools.

By the time Solecki left the Shanidar Cave for the last time, it had already revealed plenty of fascinating evidence of human life in prehistoric times. But it is likely that the cave has far more secrets to reveal. In fact, according to one of Solecki's students, Anagnostie Agelerakis, it already has.

When he reexamined the Shanidar remains in the 1990s, Agelerakis discovered materials that were not naturally found in the area. This suggested that the cave dwellers may have traded with their neighbors. Agelerakis also noticed that many of the skeletons had bad backs, probably brought on by long hours of laboring in the fields.

Hunter-gatherers and farmers

Before the development of farming, human beings used to live by hunting wild animals, fishing, and foraging for wild plants, nuts, and berries. Anthropologists call such people hunter-gatherers. Because they had to move to wherever food was plentiful, hunter-gatherers generally did not live in permanent villages, but instead lived a nomadic lifestyle.

Beginning about 9,000 B.C. onward, human beings began to settle in particular areas and grow crops. They also tamed cattle, sheep, and pigs. This style of life, known as pastoralist, was a more efficient way of getting food, and in most areas of the world the hunter-gatherer lifestyle died out.

> These arrow- and spearheads date to a time when humans were hunter-gatherers.

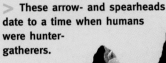

Early agriculture

Sometime around 7,000 B.C., not far from Shanidar, roughly 100 to 150 people came to live in the foothills of the Zagros Mountains. Here, on a steep hill, they built 20 permanent mud-walled houses with stone foundations. The site, known as Jarmo, was first discovered in the 1940s by the Iraqi director general of antiquities. But it was Dr. Robert Braidwood who would harvest its riches, as he dug in the mound to uncover one of the world's oldest agricultural communities.

Dr. Braidwood, who had been investigating the origins of food production, was excited by what he found. There were stone sickles used for harvesting grain and stone bowls for storing food. Together with other evidence—such as the remains of grains of emmer wheat, barley, and lentils and bones from sheep, cattle, pigs, and other farmyard animals—the tools left little doubt that the people of Jarmo were farmers.

Braidwood's excavations in Jarmo, from 1948 to 1955, provided proof that an ancient civilization had evolved from a hunting-and-gathering society to a society of farmers and herders. But it was also significant in another way. Braidwood was the first archaeologist to employ scientists from a range of different areas to help him. They included a geologist (an expert on rocks) and a zoologist (an animal specialist). By working as a team, the scientists were able to discover what ancient life in Jarmo was really like.

Meet an Archaeologist

Elizabeth Stone has always been fascinated by ancient neighborhoods and cities. In 1997, the Stony Brook University professor and her colleague Paul Zimansky uncovered the remains of a large Babylonian city. It was called Mashkan-shapir.

▣ What was the most exciting discovery you made in Iraq?

▣ In the 1980s I was leading a team to a large urban site located in the middle of the Iraqi desert. Our interest was in how this city was organized, but we did not know its name. During our first season, I was trying to identify the edges of the site when, in the middle of a dust storm, I saw a life-size human foot in baked clay on the ground. This led me to more pieces, and we wound up with about 80 pieces of the sculpture that had originally decorated the main temple. One year later, I was wandering around the site again, this time trying to trace the city wall, when I saw a number of large pieces of baked clay with cuneiform writing on them. The third piece that I looked at gave us the name of the site we were working on—Mashkan-shapir. It was a site that we knew from other inscriptions to have been briefly one of the most important Mesopotamian cities.

▣ What kinds of tools were you using?

▣ At Mashkan-shapir we wanted to understand how it was organized as a city, so we needed as broad a view as possible—which meant aerial photographs. But how were we to get them? We could not hire a helicopter (this was during the Iran-Iraq war), and there was no helium in Iraq at the time, so balloons could not be used. Our solution was to fly a kite with a camera attached. We took 1,600 photographs this way, which gave us a wonderful view of the site, showing us where the canals, streets, and much of the architecture was located.

▣ What special challenges did you face working in Iraq?

▣ Working in Iraq during the Saddam era was always complicated. We began our project at Mashkan-shapir during the Iran-Iraq war, so when in Baghdad we could hear the Iranian Scud missiles coming into the city and exploding. There were also food shortages. No coffee, no eggs, no cheese—once even no potatoes!

⏹ How does technology aid your work or provide new perspective on older finds?
⏹ Since the late 1960s, photographs have been taken of the globe using satellites. These, together with more recent images, can be used to trace the ancient canal and river systems so that we can understand the relationship between site locations and water sources. Now we have much higher resolution imagery available. Using Digital Globe imagery, we can sometimes see all of the streets and walls of ancient sites—and every hole dug into them by looters. I have been using Digital Global imagery to provide the Iraqis in the Department of Antiquities with data on sites that need to be guarded. I have also been offering training programs for the Iraqis so that they can do this themselves.

⏹ What kind of training do you recommend to kids who are interested in becoming archaeologists?
⏹ I would recommend that they become well rounded. Archaeology includes both scientists and art historians, and a field archaeologist needs some background in both areas. Kids should make sure that they like camping and the outdoor life as well. I would also visit archaeological sites, digs, and museums. Sometimes it is possible to volunteer for digs —I did this for the first time when I was eight years old.

▽ **Elizabeth Stone stands near some remains at Mashkan-shapir during an early visit to the site in the 1980s.**

The Cities of Sumer

What secrets did the royal tombs reveal?

Few excavations in the early history of archaeology have been as spectacular as that of the royal tombs at Ur, located in southern Iraq near modern Nasiriyah. When they were first discovered in the early 1900s, only the tomb of the Egyptian pharaoh Tutankhamun rivaled their importance. The royal tombs at Ur opened the world's eyes to the ancient Sumerian culture at its most magnificent.

< These steps lead to the top of the restored ziggurat at Ur. The restoration was carried out by the Iraqi Department of Antiquities.

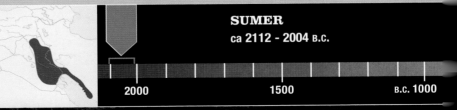

SUMER
ca 2112 - 2004 B.C.

2000   1500   B.C. 1000

Sumer

The Sumerians lived in the southernmost part of the area between the Tigris and Euphrates rivers. Beginning about 3500 B.C. Sumer was home to a number of city states. Among the most important were Ur, Nippur, Kish, Uruk, and Lagash. Each city controlled the area immediately surrounding it. There were often wars between the cities, and one would gain supremacy over the others for a while.

The city of Ur grew in wealth after 3000 B.C., and by about 2500 B.C. it was one of the most powerful cities in the region. Like other city states of the period, Ur was ruled by a king, and the economic prosperity of the city was reflected in the great riches of the royal family. The treasures of one queen, however, would remain hidden for centuries; when they were rediscovered almost 4,500 years later, they would astonish the world.

Queen Puabi

In the late 1920s, British archaeologist Charles Leonard Woolley rose to international fame when he discovered the royal tomb of Queen Puabi. Woolley was an experienced and renowned archaeologist. He worked at Ur between 1922 and 1934, often in extremely harsh conditions. During that

time Woolley and his team uncovered more than 1,800 graves. Although many of them contained valuable artifacts, 17 stood out. Woolley called them the "royal tombs." One in

V **This gold and lapis lazuli headdress was found in the tomb of Queen Puabi.**

∧ Charles Leonard Woolley brushes earth away from an ancient artifact while working on an excavation at Ur in 1925.

particular held incredible riches—the tomb of Queen Puabi. We know whom the tomb belonged to because a cylinder seal bearing the name Puabi was discovered on the body inside.

Like the tomb of King Tut, Queen Puabi's final resting place was well preserved. And so were her remains, which lay on a table, inside a chamber, inside a deep death pit.

However, it was not just the body of Puabi that was in the tomb: There were dozens of skeletons buried along with the queen. Among them were 10 handmaidens to wait on her in the afterlife and five soldiers to guard her.

> The kings and queens of Sumer entertained themselves by playing board games. This board was found with its original pieces.

In ancient Iraq, it was a great honor to serve a member of the royal family. But the honor came with a great price— servants were expected to die with their masters and mistresses.

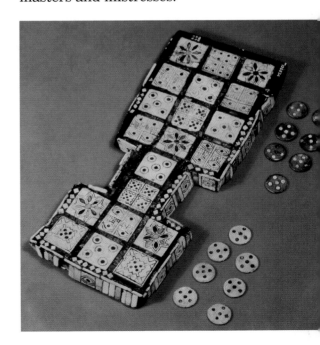

Reconstructing the Lyre of Ur

Among the many objects Leonard Woolley found at Ur were a number of lyres. The lyre is a stringed musical instrument similar to a harp. The lyres found at Ur were decorated with bulls' heads crafted in silver, bronze, and gold. One lyre belonged to the Sumerian royal family and was found with three other musical instruments.

In 2003, one of the original lyres was destroyed shortly after the outbreak of the Iraq War. On hearing of the loss, Andy Lowings, a harp enthusiast, turned to the University of Liverpool's Laser Engineering Center and asked them to create a playable replica. The engineers used lasers to engrave authentic designs onto gulf shell, a material similar to the mother of pearl that had been used to decorate the original lyre.

It was the first time the engineering team had used laser techniques on this type of material and the results were remarkable. Before reconstructing the lyre, the Liverpool engineers had used laser engraving only on materials such as plastics, metals, fabrics, and wood.

Working with extreme delicacy, the engineers were able to re-create one of the world's most fabled instruments using original materials and modern-day technology. Volunteers provided funding to buy materials for the finishing touches, including gold for the bull's head, cedar wood, lapis lazuli, and pink limestone. Now the first truly authentic reproduction of the Lyre of Ur can be played and enjoyed by music lovers.

< **This bull's head decorated the original Lyre of Ur.**

Treasures

Puabi's jewelry was fit for a queen. She wore necklaces, large earrings, and an elaborate headdress of gold leaves, gold ribbons, strands of blue lapis lazuli, and red carnelian beads. Her upper body was covered in strings of beads made from precious metals and semiprecious stones. The necklaces stretched from her shoulders to her waist. She had rings on her fingers, and more jewelry lay on the table by her head.

Many of the items found at the tombs at Ur give us glimpses into what life must have been like at court. One of the objects found in Puabi's tomb was a game board. What were the rules of the game? Did the queen spend her hours playing against her handmaidens? Another of the tomb's treasures was a magnificent lyre. When it was discovered, the fingers of one of the skeletons were still wrapped around the delicate strings. Did the skeleton perhaps belong to one of Puabi's favorite musicians, condemned to death so that she could entertain her queen in the afterlife?

Nippur

While the city of Ur yielded fantastic jewelry, another Sumerian city gave us a different kind of treasure. In ancient times Nippur was important for religious reasons; it was seen as the home of the great storm god Enlil. However, for historians its importance lies in the huge number of ancient tablets that were found there. It's largely thanks to these tablets that we know so much about the ancient Sumerians and their culture.

The first major excavation to take place at Nippur began in 1889 when a team from the University of Pennsylvania led by Hermann Hilprecht dug in an area that came to be known as Tablet Hill. Hilprecht and his colleagues worked at the site until 1900 and excavated some 60,000 tablets.

The Standard of Ur

One of the most famous and beautiful of the objects found in the royal tombs of Ur was a boxlike mosaic now known as the Standard of Ur. Originally made in about 2500 B.C., it was given its name by Leonard Woolley, who discovered it. He believed that it was carried around on a pole like a flag. The truth is that we don't know what it was used for. Another suggestion is that it was part of a musical instrument.

The mosaic, which has now been restored, was made of shell, lapis lazuli, and bitumen and was originally framed in wood. There are two main panels, one on each side of the box, showing different aspects of life in ancient Sumer. Today, historians know them as the "war" and "peace" sides. The "war" side depicts a Sumerian army, complete with war chariots. Enemy prisoners are paraded before the king of Ur. The "peace" side shows a banquet and a procession of animals.

∧ The top row of the "peace" side of the Standard of Ur shows a royal banquet. In the other rows, animals are led to slaughter.

The tablets included school lessons, multiplication tables, lists of kings, legal documents, epic tales, and astronomical records. But Hilprecht's work was only the beginning.

The next major excavation at Nippur began in 1948. It is one of the longest-running excavations in archaeological history, lasting until 1991. In the first years of the expedition, the team from the Oriental Institute of the University of Chicago concentrated on the religious center of the city. However, from 1972 onward the team took a different approach, also excavating the West Mound, a mainly residential area. Under new field director McGuire Gibson, the

< This gold and alabaster figure was found at Nippur. It is thought to be about 3,000 years old.

V Excavations are carried out at Nippur in 1952. A team from the University of Chicago worked there for over 40 years.

The Sumerian Dictionary Project

The Sumerians left us thousands of clay tablets covered in cuneiform writing. These tablets can help us learn what life was like in ancient Mesopotamia—but only if we can understand the language they were written in!

Many archaeologists have spent years studying ancient texts in an attempt to translate them. Their job is made more difficult by the fact that cuneiform—the writing system used by the ancient Mesopotamians—was used to write down several languages, in the same way that our alphabet is used to write many different languages besides English.

One person who dedicated much of his life to helping us understand Sumerian was Dr. Samuel Noah Kramer. Between 1943 and 1968 Kramer worked at the University of Pennsylvania, where he spent countless hours examining ancient clay tablets. His work paved the way for the Pennsylvania Sumerian Dictionary Project, an attempt to produce the world's first modern dictionary of the Sumerian language.

It was to prove an extremely difficult task. The project began in 1974, but it was over 30 years before the first version of the dictionary appeared on the Web. Today everyone can access the dictionary at http://psd.museum.upenn.edu/epsd. The dictionary will be updated as we learn more about the world's first written language.

team unearthed bakers' houses, a palace, and a sequence of temples. Gibson's expedition was the first to include a soil specialist on its staff. It also pioneered the use of computers for mapping, drafting, and data recording in Iraq.

The Akkadians

The age of the Sumerians ended when King Sargon of Akkad came to power in about the 24th century B.C. The reason why historians make a clear distinction between the Sumerians and the Akkadians is that they spoke different languages. The period that the

> This stele (stone pillar) celebrates the victory of King Naram-Sin of Akkad over a rival people.

The tablets of Ebla

One of the many cities conquered by the Akkadians was Ebla, now Tell-Mardikh in present-day Syria. We know quite a lot about the city of Ebla because of a vast library of clay tablets that was found there. The tablets, more than 20,000 in total, were discovered in the 1960s by two Italian archaeologists, Giovanni Pettinato and Paolo Matthiae, and were written in a Semitic language similar to that of the Akkadians. The tablets tell us a great deal about the economic life of the city. By the 24th century B.C. Ebla was flourishing, trading in timber, textiles, and agricultural produce. However, the city was destroyed by the Akkadians, either by King Sargon himself, or by his grandson Naram-Sin.

< Archaeologist Paolo Matthiae photographs a cuneiform tablet found at Tell-Mardikh. Many such tablets were discovered at the site.

Akkadians ruled Mesopotamia was relatively short—about 150 years—but the Akkadian language continued to be used for years after that.

Although he is one the most important of all Mesopotamian kings, the details of Sargon's ancestry are shrouded in mystery. One legend tells us that Sargon was raised by a gardener, who found him floating in a basket on a river. This story has great similarities to that of Moses, told in the Bible.

We don't know much about Sargon's early life, but we do know quite a lot about his achievements as a ruler. The source of our knowledge is a clay tablet that was found at Nippur during Hermann Hilprecht's original excavations there in the late 19th century. The clay tablet was a copy of an inscription on a pillar inside the temple of the god Enlil at Nippur. The inscription describes a ruthless military leader who managed to carve out a mighty empire.

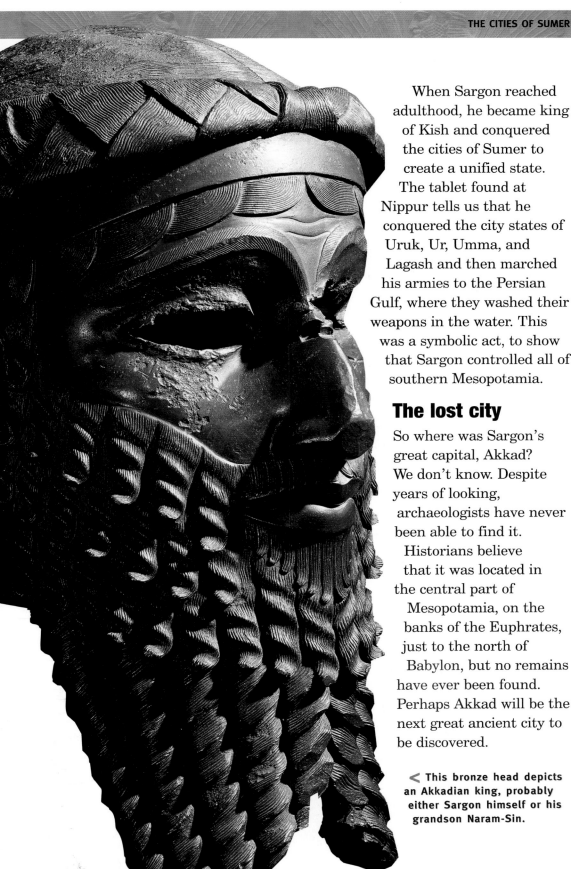

When Sargon reached adulthood, he became king of Kish and conquered the cities of Sumer to create a unified state. The tablet found at Nippur tells us that he conquered the city states of Uruk, Ur, Umma, and Lagash and then marched his armies to the Persian Gulf, where they washed their weapons in the water. This was a symbolic act, to show that Sargon controlled all of southern Mesopotamia.

The lost city

So where was Sargon's great capital, Akkad? We don't know. Despite years of looking, archaeologists have never been able to find it. Historians believe that it was located in the central part of Mesopotamia, on the banks of the Euphrates, just to the north of Babylon, but no remains have ever been found. Perhaps Akkad will be the next great ancient city to be discovered.

< This bronze head depicts an Akkadian king, probably either Sargon himself or his grandson Naram-Sin.

The Hanging Gardens

CHAPTER 4

Did one of the Wonders of the World really exist?

Before war broke out in Iraq in 2003, the ancient site of Babylon, located about 55 miles (90 km) south of Baghdad, was one of Iraq's most popular tourist sites—and one of the world's most famous ancient cities. It is perhaps best known for its hanging gardens, one of the Seven Wonders of the Ancient World. But did these gardens really exist?

During Akkadian times (from about 2300 to 2150 B.C.) Babylon was just a small village, but over the

◁ The walls that once protected the ancient city of Babylon were decorated with images of bulls and dragons.

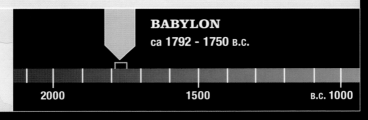

BABYLON
ca 1792 - 1750 B.C.

| 2000 | 1500 | B.C. 1000 |

∧ The cuneiform writing on this cone commemorates the building of a wall by the Babylonian king Hammurabi.

following centuries it grew in size and importance. In about 1900 B.C. it became the center of a small state ruled by a king called Sumuabum, from the Amorite people. The greatest of the Amorite kings was Hammurabi, who ruled from 1790 until 1750 B.C. Hammurabi conquered the nearby states to create a kingdom that stretched over much of Mesopotamia.

∧ The horned dragon was the symbol of Marduk, the chief god of Babylon. This bronze head was made in about the sixth century B.C.

In the first year of his reign, Hammurabi fulfilled a promise to the Babylonian god Marduk and established a new code of laws that covered nearly every area of life. He had the laws carved onto an enormous piece of black stone called a stele. The stele was seven and a half feet (2.3 m) tall and weighed several tons. Hammurabi's Code included almost 300 laws. One of the most famous says, "An eye for an eye, a tooth for a tooth." When we use this phrase today, we mean that the punishment should roughly fit the crime. In Hammurabi's time, however, somebody who blinded an enemy would actually be blinded themselves as a punishment. Babylon was a tough place to be a criminal!

Babylon was taken over by the Kassites around 1570 B.C., and for the next thousand years it was ruled by a number of different peoples. Babylon's greatest splendor came during the reign of Nebuchadnezzar II, who ruled between about 605 and 561 B.C. The reign of Nebuchadnezzar is best known for his

Hammurabi's stele

In the winter of 1901, French archaeologists J. De Morgan and Father Jean-Vincent Scheil discovered the stele of Hammurabi. It was found not in Babylon, where Hammurabi had left it, but in Susa, which is located in modern-day Iran. When the stele was found, it had been broken into three pieces. Scheil put them back together and spent six months translating the inscriptions that ran around its lower sections.

Today, Hammurabi's stele resides at the Louvre museum in Paris. But you don't have to go to France to see what it looks like. Replicas can be found in other museums, including the Prewitt/Allen Archaeological Museum, located at Corban College in Oregon, and the University of Chicago's Oriental Institute Museum.

> A picture of King Hammurabi decorates the top of his stele; his laws are inscribed underneath.

capture of the city of Jerusalem, which is described in the Bible, but this was just one of a number of military victories that helped him to establish a powerful kingdom centered around the city of Babylon itself.

Excavating Babylon

Much of what we know about ancient Babylon comes from the work of German architect and archaeologist Robert Koldewey. Koldewey began digging at Babylon on March 26, 1899, and continued to work at the site for the next 18 years. Koldewey's excavations weren't only important because of what they found. The archaeologist and his team from the

The Tower of Babel

The temple of Marduk in Babylon is believed by some historians to be the real-life inspiration for the biblical story of the Tower of Babel, which is told in the book of Genesis. The story attempts to explain the origin of languages and describes a great tower built on a plain in the land of Shinar, which is the biblical name for Babylonia. The similarity between the words "Babel" and "Babylon" has led many historians to suggest that the biblical tower and the temple of Marduk were one and the same, though others argue that the similarity is just a coincidence.

‹ **The story of the Tower of Babel has inspired artists throughout the ages.**

German Orient Society also adopted a revolutionary new scientific approach. After Koldewey's time, archaeologists increasingly began to realize the importance of a site's sequence of layers. Finds found at the same layer could help with contextual dating.

The temple of Marduk

One of Koldewey's most dramatic discoveries was the foundations of the temple of Marduk, a ziggurat, or terraced pyramid built, to honor the city's chief god. The ziggurat at Babylon was crowned with an astronomical observatory. The earliest ziggurats, from the Ur empire, were built with three levels, an effort to get people as close to their gods as they could. The ziggurat at Babylon had seven terraces, joined by a staircase.

The ziggurat Koldewey discovered was named Etemenaki, or the House of the Platform of Heaven and Earth. According to a clay tablet left by a scribe, its first step was 110 feet (34 m) high. Its second step was 60 feet (18.3 m) high, and its third, fourth, and fifth steps were each 20 feet (6.1 m) high. The seventh step was 50 feet (15.2 m) high. Although the scribe omitted the height of the sixth step, all totaled Etemenaki probably stood about 300 feet (91 m) high. Some people believe that the temple of Marduk provided the inspiration for

the biblical Tower of Babel, a temple built to reach into Heaven, but others dispute the claim.

Hanging Gardens

Impressive though it was, the ziggurat of Marduk wasn't the most famous of Koldewey's discoveries. One day the archaeologist uncovered the remains of an arched structure located near what looked like a well. Koldewey was ecstatic: He believed he had located

∧ Archaeologist Robert Koldewey was most famous for his work at Babylon.

∨ No one knows exactly what the Hanging Gardens looked like—but many artists have been fascinated enough to create imaginary pictures.

part of the Hanging Gardens of Babylon, one of the Seven Wonders of the Ancient World.

We know about the Hanging Gardens because they are mentioned in the works of several Greek writers, including Strabo and Diodorus Siculus, who both lived in the first century B.C. Strabo described a magnificent structure with a number of terraces built one on top of another. Stairs led to the higher levels, which were irrigated by engines that brought water from the nearby Euphrates. The gardens did not literally "hang." They

got their name from a Greek word meaning "overhanging," a reference to the many balconies and terraces.

Legend has it that the gardens were built by King Nebuchadnezzar II to cheer up Amyitis, one of his wives. She came from a green and hilly country called Media (part of present-day Iran) and did not like the dry and flat deserts around Babylon. The gardens were the king's attempt to re-create the conditions of her homeland.

Diodorus Siculus's descriptions of the gardens say that their foundations were made of stone. This was unusual for Mesopotamia, as most buildings were made of mud brick. However, the fact that the gardens were irrigated heavily meant that foundations made of mud would quickly have collapsed.

It was the stone foundations that first made Koldewey think that he had found the cellars of the fabled gardens. The well seemed to confirm his hunch. Surely this well had been used to irrigate the queen's gardens. One of the great mysteries of archaeology had been solved: The Hanging Gardens of Babylon had been found at last.

All in the imagination?

Many present-day historians and archaeologists have other ideas, however. Some have said that the site discovered by Koldewey is too far away from the Euphrates River to be the Hanging Gardens. In Strabo's

∨ These ruins were once the home of King Nebuchadnezzar II, one of the greatest of all the kings of Babylon.

The Ishtar Gate

In Nebuchadnezzar II's time the city of Babylon had eight separate entrances. The most magnificent of them was the Ishtar Gate, which was decorated with glazed blue bricks. When Robert Koldewey and his team first uncovered the gate in 1899, many of these bricks lay broken. However, the archaeologists were determined to restore the gate so that people could experience the sight that had greeted travelers to Babylon 2,500 years before.

The task of restoring the gate was carried out not in Iraq, but in Germany, where teams of experts sifted through the fragments and gradually rebuilt the gate piece by piece and brick by brick. Missing segments were replaced by replicas. The reconstruction was unveiled in

1930 in its new home, Berlin's Vorderasiatisches Museum. Since then, there have been many calls for the gate to be returned to Babylon. They have all been ignored. However, a replica of the gate has been built in Iraq.

> **This life-size reconstruction of the Ishtar Gate stands in Babylon, the home of the original.**

account, the gardens are located right by the river. Logically, the gardens would probably have been built near to what would have been the source of the water needed to irrigate them. Other archaeologists have pointed out that anyone visiting the gardens would have had to pass through the royal quarters first. Surely this would have been a serious inconvenience for the Babylonian king.

While some historians have suggested that the gardens may have been somewhere else, others have suggested that they may not even have existed. After all, even though they are described in detail by later Greek writers, these writers did not see them themselves; instead, they were just reporting what they had been told. The gardens are not mentioned at all on the countless clay tablets that were produced by the Babylonians themselves.

So, could one of the Seven Wonders of the Ancient World have been just a myth? It may take many more years of archaeological work before we know for sure.

The Queen of Assyria

CHAPTER 5

What treasures lay hidden at Nimrud?

Between the two great periods in Babylon's history, when Hammurabi laid down his laws and Nebuchadnezzar II built his spectacular palaces, a number of other civilizations dominated Mesopotamia. One of the most important was that of the Assyrians.

The Assyrians originally came from the town of Assur, on the banks of the Tigris River in northern Iraq. The great period of Assyrian history began in the ninth century B.C. with the reign of King

◁ This golden armband decorated with turquoise and other stones is as beautiful today as it was when an Assyrian queen wore it nearly three thousand years ago.

ASSYRIA
ca 858 - 824 B.C.

1500   1000   B.C. 500

Ashurnasirpal II. Soon after he came to power, Ashurnasirpal began a ruthless campaign of conquest that led to the creation of an empire that stretched from the Mediterranean Sea in the west to the Zagros Mountains in the east. And along with the new empire came a new capital—Nimrud. It was to become one of the most extraordinary cities in all of Mesopotamia.

> This statue is of the great Assyrian king Ashurnasirpal II.

Fit for a king

Nimrud (known as Kalhu in ancient times) was first excavated between 1847 and 1851 by the British archaeologist Austen Henry Layard. Nimrud was a fabulous find. Over the course of four years, Layard uncovered the walls and southern part of the Northwest Palace, the Ninurta Temple, the Southwest Palace, and the Ezida and Southeast Palaces. The Southeast Palace would later be called the Burnt Palace because of the discovery of a number of burnt ivories in it.

Massive statues of hawk-winged bulls with human heads guarded the Northwest Palace entrance. They would have been a frightening sight to anyone visiting the city at the height of the Assyrians' power.

During one of his visits, Layard hired local workmen to dig amid the debris that was most likely the public rooms of Ashurnasirpal II's palace. There he found remarkable stone wall

> Austen Henry Layard oversees excavations at Nimrud. Layard was the first archaeologist to work at the site. He discovered many of the city's major palaces.

The Nimrud ivories

Not all of the treasures found at Nimrud were made by the Assyrians themselves. Among the artifacts discovered there by archaeologist Max Mallowan were a large number of intricately carved ivories. Many had been made by artists from Phoenicia and then either given to the Assyrians as tribute or taken as plunder. Among the most famous of the Nimrud ivories were a carving of a lioness mauling a young shepherd and another of the head of a young woman that has been called the Mona Lisa of Nimrud.

> **This ivory carving of a winged sphinx dates to about 750 B.C.**

carvings that showed scenes of royal life. Layard also discovered a black obelisk, or stone pillar, erected by Shalmaneser III, who was Ashurnasirpal's successor. It stood six and a half feet (2 m) tall. At the top of the obelisk were three steps in the shape of a ziggurat. The monument commemorated the king's victories in campaigns against Assyria's enemies, and pictures of defeated rulers were engraved on its sides. They were shown bringing animals as tribute. The kings were obviously eager to impress Shalmaneser. One gift was an elephant, while another was a rhinoceros. The Assyrian king must have had quite a zoo!

< **A carving from the black obelisk of Shalmaneser II shows a hunting scene.**

History of an excavation

After Layard, there were many other archaeologists, including Hormuzd Rassam and George Smith, who carried out excavations at Nimrud. However, the site was relatively quiet until 1949, when Englishman Max Mallowan returned for work that would last until 1963. Mallowan, who had previously worked in Iraq as an assistant to Leonard Woolley, was accompanied by a team sponsored by the British School of Archaeology.

Mallowan's mission was to re-excavate the sites Layard had visited and to extend the excavations into

untouched areas of the palace. As the excavation continued, Mallowan realized that Layard had dug only along the edges of each room. So Mallowan dug not just along outside walls but inward from them, tripling the size of the area being investigated and leading to places that had not

previously been explored. The new discoveries included a magnificent acropolis (fortified hilltop) and a military complex that became known as Fort Shalmaneser.

Agatha Christie

Although Max Mallowan was a highly respected archaeologist, he was not nearly as famous as one of his assistants—his wife, mystery writer Agatha Christie. Christie accompanied her husband when he traveled on expeditions and helped him with his work. When Mallowan discovered the Nimrud ivories, Christie suggested that he should cover them with her hand cream to protect them from drying out. It worked!

Christie found ancient Iraq so inspiring that she set one of her novels there. *Murder in Mesopotamia* features the detective Hercule Poirot, who is called in to solve a murder that has taken place at an archaeological dig. The novel was later turned into a TV movie. Christie also wrote a factual account of her experiences in the Middle East, *Come, Tell Me How You Live*.

∧ **Max Mallowan and Agatha Christie leave their London home at the start of a journey to Iraq in 1933.**

Treasures of the queens

For decades no major new discoveries were made at Nimrud. Then, in 1989, word got out that Iraqi archaeologists had made an amazing breakthrough. The find, made by Muzahim Mahmoud Hussein, head of the team from Iraq's Department of Antiquities, turned out to be one of the most extraordinary archaeological discoveries of all time.

Hussein's first discovery came when he and his team found what looked like a slab of stone covered in dirt. On further inspection it became clear that this was the roof of a small tomb. The tomb contained a sarcophagus (stone coffin), and when Hussein pried off the lid, he was confronted by a vision of gold.

The gold was draped around the skeleton of a woman, who turned out to be Queen Yabahya. She was the wife of the Assyrian king Tiglath-Pileser III, who ruled in the eighth century B.C. In addition to the jewelry she wore, gold rosettes were scattered over Yabahya's skeleton and a gold bowl was inscribed with her name. Other bowls carried the names Atalia, the wife of Sargon II, and Banitu, the wife of Shalmaneser V. These kings ruled immediately after Tiglath-Pileser, so the bowls must have been put in the tomb at a later date.

Months later, Hussein made yet another find—a small tomb that contained only dust. It was alongside this tomb that Hussein struck gold— literally. There he found three bronze containers. Together, they held some 440 pieces of gold jewelry, weighing a total of 48.5 pounds (22kg). Archaeologists believe that these jewels may have been the private collection of an Assyrian queen.

Changed perceptions

The discovery of Yabahya's tomb has had a great impact on the way that historians view the Assyrians. Previously, they were mainly seen as great and fearsome warriors who struck terror in their many enemies. This was certainly the case. However, Hussein's discoveries have shown that the Assyrians were also highly skilled craftspeople capable of creating incredibly beautiful and delicate jewelry.

The queen's curse

Queen Yabahya's tomb was filled with surprises—not the least of which was a curse inscribed on a marble slab near the entrance. The curse threatened an eternity of sleeplessness and terrible thirst to anyone who dared remove the queen from her tomb, lay a hand on her jewelry, or break the tomb's seal. Did this mean that Hussein would be cursed forever? Probably not, as it seems that several people had already entered the tomb by the time Hussein found it. A second body lay near Queen Yabahya's. Archaeologists believe that the tomb was reopened a few years after Yabahya's death so that someone else could be buried there.

∨ **This glistening crown is one of the many treasures found at Nimrud. The face of a museum worker is reflected in its glass case.**

Protecting the Past

CHAPTER 6

How do we save the treasures of Iraq?

As we have seen, Iraq was home to some of the world's greatest ancient civilizations and the source of some of its most amazing treasures. Over the years, more than 10,000 sites of archaeological significance have been identified. Some are as small as a backyard, others are as large as an entire town. Each one is unique and has its own stories to tell. Each one is irreplaceable. And each one is endangered.

In the last decade of the 20th century and the first years of the 21st, war took its toll on Iraq's ancient sites and monuments. During the 1991 Gulf

◁ A U.S. tank protects Iraq's National Museum in Baghdad from the looting that occurred after the fall of Saddam Hussein's government.

53

War, Ur was bombed, and its great ziggurat was shaken and damaged. Military trenches were built on unexcavated tells, damaging them.

In the years following the war, Iraq suffered from increasing poverty, and the looting of ancient sites became a widespread problem. Palaces at Nimrud and Nineveh and temples at Hatra were stripped of their

∧ This wall from an Assyrian royal palace at Nineveh has been badly damaged by looters removing carvings.

sculptures. Thieves used bulldozers and dump trucks to carry away loot from raids on other sites.

Fall of the museum

The situation got worse in the early years of the 21st century. The breakdown in law and order that followed the start of the Iraq War and the fall of Saddam Hussein's government in 2003 left many of Iraq's great treasures unguarded. In April 2003, the world watched in shock as the National Museum was looted. Thousands of artifacts were stolen from their glass cases. Larger pieces were broken up so that they could be carried away.

In the days that followed the looting of the museum, there was massive confusion about the scale of the disaster. How many pieces had disappeared? Could it really be as many as 170,000, as some newspapers were claiming? And which pieces were missing and which ones were safe? If the museum's catalogs were destroyed in the chaos, could we ever really know?

It soon became clear that the extent of the thefts had been exaggerated. Many of the pieces that everybody thought had been stolen were in fact safely hidden away by museum staff. Gradually, the number of looted artifacts came down. Soon, newspaper articles were saying that only 15,000 pieces were missing. But while historians and archaeologists were pleased that the disaster wasn't as bad as was once thought, they knew that the situation was still bad: 15,000 articles was a massive loss. Especially as the number included such famous

> Archaeologists McGuire Gibson (left) and Henry Wright examine objects that were returned to Iraq's National Museum shortly after it was looted.

∨ An Iraqi worker stands next to a broken ancient statue in his country's National Museum. Many priceless artifacts have been damaged during the Iraq War.

The Warka Vase

One of the most famous objects to be looted from Baghdad's National Museum was the Warka Vase. At about 5,000 years old, it is the earliest carved stone vase in existence. The carving shows aspects of early Mesopotamian life. The scenes include a procession of domesticated animals.

When the vase disappeared, archaeologists were worried that it might never be seen again. However, in June 2003 three men turned up unexpectedly at the gates of the National Museum, opened the trunk of their car, and simply handed the vase over. It had been broken into several pieces, but experts are confident that it can be restored.

pieces as the Bassetki Statue, a copper figure dating to about 2200 B.C., and the Warka Vase.

Retrieving the treasures

Faced with the tremendous losses caused by the looting of the National Museum, many of the world's most famous archaeological institutions decided to try to help. One was the University of Chicago's Oriental Institute. The Oriental Institute has a long relationship with Iraq. A team from the department worked at the Sumerian city of Nippur for over 40 years.

In April 2003, shortly after the initial looting, the Institute created an online database that aimed to list all the objects that were known to be held at the National Museum before war broke out. The site, which can be accessed at http://oi.uchicago.edu/OI/IRAQ/dbfiles/Iraqdatabasehome.htm, tells us which objects are believed to be stolen and which are safe. The Institute updates the status of artifacts as they are recovered or determined to be missing. The archaeologists behind the database hope that it will help people find and return stolen items to the museum.

Rescue mission

The Oriental Institute wasn't the only organization to offer aid. The National Geographic Society also took significant steps to assist the recovery effort in Iraq. In May 2003, it dispatched an expedition to Iraq to survey key archaeological sites.

< This is what the Warka Vase looked like before it was stolen and broken into pieces.

> **U.S. soldiers pose in front of an ancient Babylonian statue shortly after the beginning of the Iraq War in 2003.**

It also sent a team of experts on another very important mission—to rescue treasures from the royal tombs at Nimrud and the royal cemetery at Ur that had been stashed in the underground vaults at Baghdad's Central Bank since before the Gulf War.

Several floors of the bank had been looted in the days after the outbreak of the Iraq War, but this wasn't the main danger facing the treasures. The vaults, located in the bank's cellar, had been flooded by water overflowing from the Tigris River. The bank was flooded right up to ground level.

Rescuing the treasures was a major task. It took three pumps running nonstop for three weeks to get the water out from the cellars. In all, over half a million gallons (1.9 million liters) of water had to be removed. When the cellar was finally drained, the boxes that contained the treasures were found.

But were the treasures safe inside? Had they survived Saddam Hussein's regime, U.S. missile strikes, and other catastrophes only to be destroyed by sewage and foul water? No one knew the answer, until the archaeologist who had originally sealed the boxes confirmed that the seals were still intact. When the boxes were opened, the bank employees stood by to verify the findings and the listing of their contents. All of the treasures were undamaged.

Lost and found

Thanks to these efforts and others, thousands of looted or misplaced artifacts have been returned to Iraq's National Museum. They range from tiny cylinder seals to famed artworks like the statue of King Entemena of Lagash, which was retrieved by U.S. officials after being smuggled across the Syrian border. Despite these successes, however, considerable difficulties remain for archaeologists determined to save the treasures of Iraq's rich past.

The Years Ahead

In the months and years immediately following the downfall of Saddam Hussein's government, one of the key figures involved in protecting Iraq's antiquities was Donny George. He had been director of the National Museum before the war and continued to work there after the U.S. intervention. In August 2006, George was forced to leave the country because of the increasing danger. Before he left, he sealed off the museum with concrete walls in one last desperate attempt to protect its priceless contents from looters.

Despite the problems caused by the lack of law and order in the country, archaeologists from Iraq and around the world will continue to do all they can to protect Iraq's incredible heritage. Maybe one day, when the violence ends, George will be able to return to a reopened museum. People will again walk through the amazing galleries and talk of the place where civilization was born.

< Donny George, former director of the Iraq National Museum, is pictured with two of the country's treasures.

Glossary

acropolis – a raised, fortified part of a city

afterlife – an existence after death

antiquities – relics or artifacts from ancient times

archaeologist – a person who studies the material remains of an ancient culture

artifact – any object changed by human activity

bitumen – a natural substance used as cement or tar

carbon dating – a way of dating an object by measuring how much the carbon-14 within it has decayed

cemetery – a place where a number of dead bodies are buried

circa – about; used to indicate a date that is approximate, and abbreviated as ca

citadel – a stronghold or fortress

city state – a single town or city that governs the region immediately around it

code – a set of laws

contextual dating – a way of dating an object by comparing its age with that of the objects found near it

cuneiform – an ancient system of writing that uses wedge-shaped characters

cylinder seal – a cylinder that is rolled in wet clay to produce a kind of signature

excavation – an archaeological dig

foraging – looking for food

hunter-gatherer – a member of a culture that gets its food by hunting and foraging rather than growing crops and raising animals

lapis lazuli – a semiprecious stone that is a rich blue in color and often used in jewelry

looting – stealing objects during a breakdown in law and order

lyre – a musical instrument similar to a harp

Mesopotamia – the area of Iraq that lies between the Tigris and Euphrates Rivers

minaret – a slender tower attached to a mosque

Neanderthal – a forerunner of the modern human being. The Neanderthals inhabited Europe and Asia until about 30,000 B.C.

Neolithic – belonging to the Stone Age

nomad – a member of a people who have no fixed home and move from place to place

obelisk – a stone pillar, usually with four sides and a pyramid-shaped top

pastoralism – a style of life based around the raising of livestock

prehistoric – relating to the period of time before written history

sarcophagus – a stone coffin

sounding – an investigative technique undertaken by archaeologists to test conditions at various depths

sphinx – a creature with the head of a person but the body of a lion

stele – a commemorative stone pillar

tablet – a slab, usually made of clay or stone, carrying an inscription

tell – an earth mound containing ancient artifacts

tomb – a place where a dead body is laid to rest

ziggurat – a step-sided pyramid used as a temple

Bibliography

Books

Haywood, John. *Ancient Civilizations of the Near East and Mediterranean*. Armonk, NY: Sharpe Reference, 1997.

Mesopotamia: The Mighty Kings (Lost Civilizations). Alexandria, VA: Time-Life Books, 1995.

Sumer: Cities of Eden (Lost Civilizations). Alexandria, VA: Time-Life Books, 1993.

Articles

Lawler, Andrew. "Beyond the Looting: What's Next for Iraq's Treasures." NATIONAL GEOGRAPHIC (October 2003): 58–75.

Web Sites

Handwerk, Brian. "Hunt for Stolen Iraqi Treasures Moves to Cyperspace." NATIONAL GEOGRAPHIC NEWS
http://nationalgeographic.com/news/2003/04/0429_030429_iraqlooting.html

Williams, Jason. "Ancient Assyrian Treasures Found Intact in Baghdad." NATIONAL GEOGRAPHIC NEWS
http://nationalgeographic.com/news/2003/06/0602_030602_iraqgold.html

Further Reading

Bancroft Hunt, Norman. *Historical Atlas of Ancient Mesopotamia*. New York: Checkmark Books, 2004.

McIntosh, Jane. *Ancient Mesopotamia: New Perspectives*. Santa Barbara, CA: ABC-CLIO, 2005.

Oakes, Lorna, and Philip Steele. *Everyday Life in Ancient Egypt and Mesopotamia*. London: Southwater, 2006.

Schomp, Virginia. *Ancient Mesopotamia: The Sumerians, Babylonians, and Assyrians*. New York: Franklin Watts, 2005.

On the Web

Iraq National Museum
http:www.baghdadmuseum.org/home.php

Mesopotamia (The British Museum)
http://www.mesopotamia.co.uk

Mesopotamia (Washington State University)
http://www.wsu.edu/~dee/MESO/MESO.htm

Royal Tombs of Ur (Oriental Institute, University of Chicago)
http://oi.uchicago.edu/OI/UR/Ur_home.html

Index

Boldface indicates illustrations.

About the Author

BETH GRUBER has worked in children's publishing for more than 20 years as an author, editor, and reviewer of books for young readers. A graduate of the New York University School of Journalism, she is the author of National Geographic's *Countries of the World: Mexico* and *National Geographic Investigates: Ancient Inca*, among other titles.

About the Consultant

TONY WILKINSON originally trained as a geographer at the University of London and at McMaster University in Hamilton, Ontario. He then moved into archaeology and began to work on regional landscape projects in the United Kingdom and the Near East. He was assistant director of the British Archaeological Expedition to Iraq during the late 1980s. Wilkinson is currently a professor at the Department of Archaeology, Durham University, England, where he specializes in the study of the archaeology of landscape, specifically of the ancient Near East.

< This statue of a ram climbing through a thicket was found in the royal cemetery at Ur. It is partially made of gold and dates to about 2500 B.C.

One of the world's largest nonprofit scientific and educational organizations, the National Geographic Society was founded in 1888 "for the increase and diffusion of geographic knowledge." Fulfilling this mission, the Society educates and inspires millions every day through its magazines, books, television programs, videos, maps and atlases, research grants, the National Geographic Bee, teacher workshops, and innovative classroom materials. The Society is supported through membership dues, charitable gifts, and income from the sale of its educational products. This support is vital to National Geographic's mission to increase global understanding and promote conservation of our planet through exploration, research, and education.

For more information, please call 1-800-NGS-LINE (647-5463) or write to the following address:

National Geographic Society
1145 17th Street N.W.
Washington, D.C. 20036-4688
U.S.A.

Visit the Society's Web site:
www.nationalgeographic.com

Library of Congress Cataloging-in-Publication Data available upon request
Hardcover ISBN-10: 0-7922-5382-5
ISBN-13: 978-0-7922-5382-2
Library Edition ISBN-10: 0-7922-5383-3
ISBN-13: 978-0-7922-5383-9

Printed in Mexico

Series design by Jim Hiscott
The body text is set in Century Schoolbook
The display text is set in Helvetica Neue, Clarendon

National Geographic Society

John M. Fahey, Jr., *President and Chief Executive Officer;* Gilbert M. Grosvenor, *Chairman of the Board;* Nina D. Hoffman, *Executive Vice President, President of Book Publishing Group*

Staff for This Book

Nancy Laties Feresten, *Vice President, Editor-in-Chief of Children's Books*
Virginia Ann Koeth, *Project Editor*
Bea Jackson, *Director of Design and Illustration*
Lori Epstein, Greta Arnold, National Geographic Image Sales, *Illustrations Editors*
Jean Cantu, *Illustrations Specialist*
Carl Mehler, *Director of Maps*

Priyanka Lamichhane, *Assistant Editor*
R. Gary Colbert, *Production Director*
Lewis R. Bassford, *Production Manager*
Vincent P. Ryan, Maryclare Tracy, Nicole Elliott, *Manufacturing Managers*

For the Brown Reference Group, plc

Chris King, *Volume Editor*
Alan Gooch, *Book Designer*
Becky Cox, *Picture Manager*
Encompass Graphics, *Cartographer*
Tim Cooke, *Managing Editor*

Photo Credits

Front cover: An ivory plaque from Nimrud thought to portray the goddess Ishtar.
Page 1 and back cover: A sitting lion made from terra-cotta in ancient Babylon.
Pages 2–3: The walls of the city of Nineveh.

NATIONAL GEOGRAPHIC I
EOGRAPHIC INVESTIGAGE
NVESTIGATES NATIONAL
ES NATIONAL GEOGRAPHI
L GEOGRAPHIC INVESTIGA
C INVESTIGATES NATION
ATES NATIONAL GEOGRA
NAL GEOGRAPHIC INVEST
PHIC INVESTIGATES NATI
GATES NATIONAL GEOGR
ONAL GEOGRAPHIC INVES
RAPHIC INVESTIGATES NA
STIGATES NATIONAL GEO
ATIONAL GEOGRAPHIC IN
OGRAPHIC INVESTIGATES
NVESTIGATES NATIONAL
S NATIONAL GEOGRAPHIC